Islam Quiz 300 Questions Answers

WBwinner Publishing

Published by WBwinner Publishing, 2024.

While every precaution has been taken in the preparation of this book, the publisher assumes no responsibility for errors or omissions, or for damages resulting from the use of the information contained herein.

ISLAM QUIZ 300 QUESTIONS ANSWERS

First edition. February 15, 2024.

Copyright © 2024 WBwinner Publishing.

ISBN: 979-8224604456

Written by WBwinner Publishing.

Table of Contents

ISLAM QUIZ

300

QUESTIONS

ANSWERS

Introduction

About Islam

Islam is an Abrahamic religion. It takes part of the continuity of the Jewish and Christian religions. It leans on the dogma of absolute Monotheism and takes its source from the Holy Koran, which is considered as the Word of God's receptacle. This was revealed to Muhammad who is the last prophet of God in Arabia in the 7th century.

About this book

This book "Islam Quiz 300 Questions-Answers" is a book of general knowledge on the religion of Islam. It is a brilliant idea to initiate and improve your knowledge in Islam. It is an opportunity for children as well as adults not only to entertain themselves but also to expand their knowledge in Islam.

Content of this book

Thanks to this book, you can test your knowledge, play quizzes alone, with friends or family. This quiz consists of a series of 300 questions for which there is only one right option.

Characteristics of this book:

✓ 300 Questions Answers.

✓ With solutions at the end of the book.

✓ 4 Themes: The Holy Koran - The Prophet Muhammad - The prophets – General knowledge in Islam.

✓ Size: 21.59×27.94 cm (Nearly A4)

THEME 1: The Holy Koran

1- The first word revealed in the Koran " Iqraa" means:

A) pray

B) read

C) obey me

2- The word Koran means

A) Wisdom

B) Reading

C) Submission

3- What was the first language of the original version of The Holy Koran?

A) French

B) English

C) Arabic

4- A surah of the Koran is a set of:

A) letters

B) verses

C) Islamic teachings

5- The Holy Koran contains

A) 99 suras

B) 111 suras

C) 114 suras

6- How many Hizbs are there in the Koran?

A) 100

B) 60

C) 50

7- The revelation of the Koran was spread over:

A) 10 years

B) 15 years

C) 23 years

8- The revelation of the Koran took place in:

A) Mecca

B) Mecca and Medina

C) Mecca and in Mesopotamia

9- The revelations were done:

A) by surah

B) by 2 verses

C) in a variable way

10- The Holy Koran contains several parts (juz'). How many?

A) 30

B) 50

C) 70

11- Reading a Surah is equivalent to reading one third of the Holy Koran. Which one?

A) Al-Ikhlaas

B) Al-Fatiha

C) Al-Baqarah

12- Which sura includes The Verse of Throne (Ayat al Kursi), known for its power of protection and healing?

A) Al-Baqarah

B) Al-Isra'a

13- The first sura of the Holy Koran is

A) Al-Fatiha

B) Al Baqarah

C) Al Hajj

14- The Holy Koran was revealed to the prophet (pbuh) during the month of :

A) Ramadan

B) Safar

C) Muharram

15- The Koran is the word of :

A) Gabriel

B) Allah

C) Muhammad

16- The Koran was descended to Muhammad (pbuh) by the angel ...

A) Israfil

B) Mikhail

C) Jibril (Gabriel)

17- How many verses are there in the Koran?

A) 4444

B) 6346

C) 5555

18- In the Koran, it was written that Allah pardons everyone except

A) Hypocrites

B) Polytheists

19- Which sura is the shortest one in the Koran?

A) Al-Baqarah

B) Al-Insan

C) Al-Kawthar

20- The longest sura in the Koran is ...

A) Al Maida'a

B) Al Baqarah

C) Al Nissa

21- Which one is the only sura that does not contain "bismillah al Rahman al Rahim" at the beginning?

A) At-Tawbah

B) Maryam

22- The prophet who was mentioned 139 times in the Koran is ...

A) Ibrahim (Abraham)

B) Musa (Moses)

C) Issa (Jesus)

23- Which suras are full of light (Azzahrawen)?

A) Al-Baqarah & Aal-Imran

B) Al-Baqarah & At-Tawba

C) Al-Nisa'a & Aal-Imran

24- Does The Koran only address Arabs?

A) Yes

B) No, the whole mankind

C) Only the men

25- How many Meccan suras and Medina suras is the Koran composed of?

A) 100 Meccan suras et 14 Medina suras

B) 86 Meccan suras et 28 Medina suras

26- How many words does the Holy Koran consist of?

A) 88439

B) 77439

C) 99439

27- How many letters are there in the Koran?

A) 323670

B) 556892

C) 725874

28- How many "Sajda" does the Koran consist of?

A) 10

B) 12

C) 14

29- A sura bears the name of one of the pillars of Islam.
Which one?

A) At-Tawba

B) Al-Hajj

C) Aal Imran

30- Which sura was named after one of the names of the Koran?

A) Al-Forqan

B) Al-Tawba

C) Al-Nour

31- A sura bears the name of a woman. Which one?

A) Mariem (Mary)

B) Rouquaya

C) Fatima

32- A sura contains bismillah twice. Which one?

A) Al Nour (la lumière)

B) Al Namel (les fourmis)

C) At-Tawba (Le repentir)

33- Which sura is named after one of the days of the week?

A) Al Baquarah

B) Al A'araf

C) Al Joumou'a (Friday)

34- Two surahs indicate two prayer times. Which ones?

A) Al Sobeh et Al Dhur

B) Al Maghreb et Al I'cha

C) Al Fajr et Al A'ser

35- A surah bears the name of a fruit. Which one?

A) Al-Tin (fig)

B) Al-Kawthar

C) Al-Ikhlas

36- A surah bears the name of a river. Which one?

A) Al Kawther

B) Al Ma'oun

C) Al Falaq

37- Which surah bears the name of a planet?

A) Al-Kamar (Moon)

B) Al-Shams (Sun)

C) Al-Najm (Star)

38- How many words does "Ayat al Kursi" contain?

A) 30

B) 40

C) 50

39- Where were revealed the first verses of the Koran?

A) in the cave of Hira in Mecca

B) in Jerusalem

C) in Medina

40- Which sura equals to one fourth of the Koran ?

A) Al-Kafiroun

B) Al-Ma'oun

41- A surah that initiates the Holy Koran is...

A) Al-Fatiha (The Opening)

B) Al-Nisaa (The Women)

C) Al-Baquara (The Cow)

42- When was the Koran revealed to the prophet Muhammad (pbuh)?

A) at the night of Destiny

B) at Aid-Al-Adhha (the festival of Sacrifice)

C) on the 10th day of Muharram

43- Which surah is called "the half of the Koran"?

    A) Al-Zalzala (The Earthquake)

    B) Al-Moutafifin (The dealers in Fraud)

    C) Al-Houmaza (The Scandalmongers)

44- Which surah finished with two names of prophets?

    A) Al-Nassr (The Victory)

    B) Al-Massad (The Palm Fiber)

    C) Al-A'ala (The All-Highest)

45- Which surah did not begin with bismillah?

    A) At-Tawba (The Repentance)

    B) A-Ikhlas (The Purity of Faith)

    C) Al-Anbia'a (The prophets)

46- Which surah was revealed complete?

    A) Al-Mudather (The Cloaked One)

    B) Al-Ma'idah (The Table)

    C) Al-Anbia'a (The prophets)

47- A Surah is named after one of the prophet's battles. Which one?

    A) Al-Ahzeb (The Clans)

    B) Al-Israa (The Night Journey)

48- Which surah was revealed to the prophet after his migration to Medina?

    A) Al-Anfal (The Spoils of War)

    B) Taha

    C) Al-Baqarah (The Cow)

49- Which numbers are the most repeated in the Holy Koran?

    A) 1 - 7

    B) 5 - 11

    C) 100 - 300

50- Which surah finished with the same word as its name?

     A) Al Kafiroun (The Disbelievers)

     B) Al Nas (The Mankind)

     C) Al Sharh (The Solace)

THEME 2 : The Prophet Muhammad

51- Where was Muhammad born?

A) in Medina

B) in Mecca

C) in Jerusalem

52- When did Muhammad live?

A) IV-V century

B) VI-VII century

C) VIII-IX century

53- What was the job of Muhammad?

A) Doctor

B) Shepherd

C) Lawyer

54- Who was his first wife?

A) Khadija

B) Fatima

C) Sarah

55- Where did Muhammad take refuge after his escape from Mecca?

A) Medina

B) Jerusalem

C) Damascus

56- Which people does Mouhammad take part of?

A) The Byzantines

B) The Francs

C) The Arabs

57- Where did Muhammad receive the word of God for the first time?

A) The Heet Cave

B) The Hira Cave

C) The Thor Cave

58- How do we call the successors of Muhammad?

A) Caliphs

B) Emirs

C) Sultans

59- He heard ...

A) The words of Jesus

B) The words of his father

C) The words of Allah

60- Did Muhammad know his parents?

A) Yes

B) No, he was an orphan

C) Maybe

61- The prophet Muhammad (pbuh) was born in

A) 600 A.D

B) 570 A.D

62- What is the name of Muhammad's father?

A) Abde Allah

B) Abou Bakr

63- Which one is the name of Muhammad's mother?

A) Amina

B) Khadija

C) Fatima

64- Did Muhammad's father die before or after the birth of the prophet Muhammad (pbuh)?

A) before his birth

B) after his birth

65- The mother of the prophet Muhammad (pbuh) passed

away when Muhammad was six years old?

A) True

B) False

66- The prophet Muhammad (pbuh) was eight years old when his grandfather died?

A) True

B) False

67- Which one is the name of the prophet's wet nurse?

A) Aïcha

B) Halima

68- Muhammad travelled to Cham (= Now Syria and parts of the neighboring countries) for the first time with his uncle at the age of ten?

A) True

B) False

69- After the death of his mother, he was adopted by his grandfather and then by his uncle.

A) True

B) False

70- The prophet started working as a shepherd

A) True

B) False

71- How old was he when Angel Jibril (Gabriel) first visited him?

A) 30

B) 35

C) 40

72- Which one of these three people is the cousin of the prophet?

A) Abou Baker Sedik

B) Ali Ibn Abi Talib

C) Othmane Ibn Affene

73- The name of Muhammad's father is ...

A) Abdel Muttalib

B) Abdellah

C) Ibrahim

74- Who is not the uncle of the prophet?

A) Hamza

B) Abbes

C) Abou Oubayda

75- The prophet had...

A. 4 daughters et 3 sons (Fatima, Zeyneb, Roukaya, Oum Kalthoum, Quassim, Ibrahim, Abdellah)

B) 7 daughters et 2 sons

C) 10 daughters et 4 sons

76- Who fostered the prophet successively after the death of his parents?

A) Abdul Muttalib then Abou Talib

B) Abbes then Abou Talib

C) Hamza then Abou Talib

77- Which children did the prophet bring up?

A) Talha and Zoubayr

B) Al-Mughira and Muawiya

C) Ali and Zayd Ibn Haritha

78- Who is not one of the prophet's daughters?

A) Zeyneb

B) Roukaya

C) Maymouna

79-   The prophet was buried next to ...

A) Abu Bakr and Omar

B) Othmane and Ali

C) Zeyneb and Fatima

80-   What are the names of the prophet's parents?

A) Jaafer and Hafsa

B) Omar and Halima

C) Abdullah and Amina

81-   At what age did he marry Khadija?

A) 30

B) 25

C) 40

82-   How much time did he stay in Mecca before his migration?

A) 7

B) 9

C) 13

83-   What was his first battle?

A) Badr

B) Uhud

84-   Shall we love the prophet more than our own family?

A) Yes

B) No

85-   How old was the prophet when the first signs of prophecy were discovered?

A) Since his birth

B) 6 years old by his uncle Abu Talib

C) 12 years old by a monk named Bahira

86- During how much time the call to Islam was done secretly?

A) 5 years

B) 3 years

C) 1 year

87- Which miracle did he bring to mankind?

A) The Koran

B) The Gospel

C) The Torah

88- Which house was the prophet buried in?

A) Fatima

B) Aicha

C) Khadija

89- Which tribe does the prophet belong to?

A) Kouraych

B) Badr

C) Uhud

90- What was the name of the last battle where the prophet attended?

A) Badr

B) Tabuk

C) Hunayn

91- What is the name of the mountain where the Hira Cave is situated?

A) Uhud

B) Al-Nur

C) Arafa

92- Who was the last wife of the prophet Muhammad?

A) Hafsa

B) Zeyneb

C) Maymouna

93- How many battles did the prophet attend?

A) 18

B) 27

C) 35

94- Which food is the most eaten by the prophet?

A) dates and water

B) bread

C) meat

95- How many times did the prophet go on a pilgrimage during his entire life?

A) 1

B) 3

C) 5

96- After ten years of his mission, the prophet lost two important people. Who are they?

A) his sons Qassim et Abdullah

B) his uncle Abu Talib and his wife Khadija

C) his grandfather Abdul Muttalib and his uncle Abu Talib

97- Who is the most harmful person to the prophet?

A) Abu Lahab

B) Abu Sofien

C) Muawiya

98- What were the prophet's companions doing after 5 years of his mission?

A) They built a mosque in Medina

B) They said goodbye to their families

C) They migrated to Al Habacha (Abyssinia)

99- The prophet went on two great trips. Which ones?

A) Mecca and Medina

B) Israa et Miraj

C) Cham et Egypt

100- The prophet passed away at

A) 50

B) 63

C) 70

THEME 3: The prophets

101- Which prophet had the most detailed and beautiful story in the Koran?

A) Ismail

B) Yussef (Joseph)

C) Ibrahim (Abraham)

102- Which people was the prophet Saleh (Methuselah) sent to?

A) Thamūd

B) 'Ad

C) Madyan

103- Which prophet was nicknamed the father of hosts (Abu Ad Dayfan)?

A) Nuh (Noah)

B) Ibrahim (Abraham)

C) Suleyman (Solomon)

104- Which birds did God send to Kabil (Cain) after he had killed his brother Habil (Abel)?

A) eagles

B) crows

C) swans

105- God said: « And we raised him to a high rank ». Which prophet is this?

A) Ismail (Ishmael)

B) Isa (Jesus)

C) Idris (Enoch)

106- How many stars did the prophet Yusuf see in his dream?

A) 9

B) 10

C) 11

107- Which prophet was the first one to make chainmail?

A) Dawud (David)

B) Zakariya (Zechariah)

C) Nuh (Noah)

108- Which prophet spoke to people in his cradle?

A) Ilyas (Elijah)

B) Musa (Moses)

C) Isa (Jesus)

109- Who was the Torah revealed to?

A) Isa (Jesus)

B) Musa (Moses)

C) Dawud (David)

110- How many nights since the beginning of Ramadan have the psalms been revealed to David?

A) 6

B) 12

C) 21

111- Who is the prophet with whom King Nemrod was having a discussion?

A) Suleyman (Solomon)

B) Musa (Moses)

C) Ibrahim (Abraham)

112- The richest and the most powerful prophet is..

A) Suleyman (Solomon)

B) Musa (Moses)

C) Ibrahim (Abraham)

113- The poorest prophet is ...

A) Musa (Moses)

B) Ibrahim (Abraham)

C) Issa (Jesus)

114- The prophet whose name was drawn from God Himself is ...

A) Ibrahim (Abraham)

B) Musa (Moses)

C) Muhammad

115- The prophet whose name means vitality (His parents were aged)

A) Yahya (John the Baptist)

B) Ibrahim (Abraham)

C) Isa (Jesus)

116- The most mentioned prophet in the Koran is:

A) Ibrahim (Abraham)

B) Musa (Moses)

C) Isa (Jesus)

117- The prophet who was abandoned by his ten brothers was...

A) Ibrahim (Abraham)

B) Isa (Jesus)

C) Yusuf (Joseph)

118- The prophet who was about to be sacrificed and helped to build the Kaaba is ...

A) Ismail (Ishmael)

B) Ibrahim (Abraham)

C) Yusuf (Joseph)

119- God has blessed him on the day of his birth, his death and when he will resuscitate

A) Yahya (John the Baptist)

B) Isa (Jesus)

C) Ibrahim (Abraham)

120- The prophet whose people were destroyed after a deluge of stones is ...

A) Musa (Moses)

B) Ibrahim (Abraham)

C) Lut (Lot)

121- The prophet whose people were destroyed by a deluge

A) Dawud (David)

B) Musa (Moses)

C) Nuh (Noah)

122- The prophet whose people threw him into fire

A) Ibrahim (Abraham)

B) Nuh (Noah)

C) Ismail (Ishmael)

123- Who was the first messenger on earth?

A) Nuh (Noah)

B) Adam

C) Ibrahim (Abraham)

124- Musa (Moses), Harun (Aaron), Mariam (Mary) are the children of...

A) Yaa'qub (Jacob)

B) Imran

C) Ilyas

125- Which prophet was sent to the people of 'Ad?

A) Idris (Enoch)

B) Isa (Jesus)

C) Hud (Eber)

126- Which prophet who had food coming out of his finger, when being a child?

A) Musa (Moses)

B) Shu'ayb

C) Ibrahim (Abraham)

127- Which animal was supposed to eat Yusuf (Joseph)?

A) a camel

B) a wolf

C) a cow

128- Which prophet spoke directly to Allah?

A) Ibrahim (Abraham)

B) Musa (Moses)

C) Isa (Jesus)

129- Which prophet underwent most ordeals?

A) Dawud (David)

B) Suleyman (Solomon)

C) Ayub (Job)

130- Which prophet whose the beauty equals to half of the mankind?

A) Yusef (Joseph)

B) Lut (Lot)

C) Nuh (Noah)

131- Which prophet was the friend of Allah?

A) Idris (Enoch)

B) Ibrahim (Abraham)

C) Musa (Moses)

132- Which prophet had a night journey, visited the 7 heavens and saw the prophets?

A) Ibrahim (Abraham)

B) Muhammad (pbuh)

C) Isa (Jesus)

133- Which prophet died in the 4th sky?

A) Hud

B) Imran

C) Idris (Enoch)

134- How many times did Muhammad (pbuh) see Jibril (Gabriel) in his angelic figure?

A) 7

B) 2

C) 17

135- How many prophets and messengers are there overall?

A) 100

B) 1000

C) 124000

136- Which prophet did «Bani Israel» cut into two pieces?

A) Zakaria (Zechariah)

B) Yahya (John the Baptist)

C) Musa (Moses)

137- Which prophet ate the leaves in fear of falling into the sin?

A) Musa (Moses)

B) Yahya (John the Baptist)

C) Isa (Jesus)

138- How many sons does Ya'qub (Jacob) have?

A) 11

B) 12

C) 13

139- Yaa'qub is the father of Jews

A) False

B) True

C) we don't know

140- Who is the father of the prophets?

A) Adam

B) Ibrahim (Abraham)

C) Muhammad

141- Who is our teacher on earth?

A) Adam

B) Muhammad

C) Isa (Jesus)

142- Today, we are the children of ...

A) Adam

B) Muhammad

C) Ibrahim (Abraham)

143- There is a rock in Palestine where were killed ...

A) 50 prophets

B) 70 prophets

C) 100 from Bani Israël

144- The prophets are all messengers

A) False

B) True

C) We don't know

145- Which prophet made the believers cross the Red Sea and saved them from Pharaoh?

A) Nuh (Noah)

B) Ibrahim (Abraham)

C) Musa (Moses)

146- Which prophet was evicted from his house by his 11 brothers by jealousy and was bought as a slave in Egypt?

A) Yahya (John the Baptist)

A) Yusuf (Joseph)

B) Nuh (Noah)

147- Who is the prophet Isa?

A) Jesus, son of Mary

B) Musa (Moses)

C) Ibrahim (Abraham)

148- Which prophet built an ark to gather the believers In God?

A) Idriss (Enoch)

B) Ismaïl (Ishmael)

C) Nuh (Noah)

149- Which prophets built "Al-Kaaba" in Mecca?

A) Ayub (Jacob) et Idris (Enoch)

B) Ibrahim (Abraham) et Ismail (Ishmael)

C) Nuh (Noah) et Saleh (Methuselah)

150- Which prophet was the cousin of the prophet Yahya (John the Baptist)?

A) Yunes (Jonah)

B) Isa (Jesus)

C) Yaa'qub (Jacob)

151- Ibrahim (Abraham) had two sons that were prophets, who are they?

A) Ismail et Is-haq (Isaac)

B) Adam et Eve

C) Yunus (Jonah) et Hud (Eber)

152- Which prophet underwent the affliction of a long and painful illness?

A) Muhammad

B) Saleh

C) Ayub (Job)

153- Which prophet was the son of the prophet Dawud (David)?

A) Musa (Moses)

B) Yussef (Joseph)

C) Suleyman (Solomon)

154- The miracle of the camel was granted to

A) Adam

B) Idris (Enoch)

C) Saleh

155- In Islam, who was the last prophet sent to the whole mankind?

A) Isa (Jesus)

B) Muhammad

C) Yunus (Jonah)

156- The prophet who had leprosy was ...

A) Ayub (Job)

B) Saleh

C) Adam

157- The most mentioned prophet in the Koran is

A) Muhammad

B) Musa (Moses)

C) Isa (Jesus)

158- The prophet whose people were destroyed by deluge of stones is

A) Lut (Lot)

B) Hud (Eber)

C) Dawud (David)

159- Which prophet has never lied except 3 times

A) Ibrahim (Abraham)

B) Ismail

C) Is-haq (Isaac)

160- Which prophet knew how to speak to birds?

A) Lut (Lot)

B) Dawud (David)

C) Suleyman (Solomon)

161- For how long did the prophet Ayub (Job) endure his affliction?

A) 12 years

B) 18 years

C) 21 years

162- Which prophet was a carpenter?

A) Zakaria (Zachariah)

B) Yahya (John the Baptist)

C) Is-haq (Isaac)

163- Which prophet was sent to a people who were struck by an earthquake for calling him a liar?

A) Is-haq (Isaac)

B) Yaa'qub (Jacob)

C) Shou'aib (Jethro)

164- Which prophet Ibliss refused to prostrate?

A) Adam

B) Nuh (Noah)

C) Musa (Moses)

165- Who was the first messenger?

A) Dawud (David)

B) Ibrahim (Abraham)

C) Nuh (Noah)

166- What was the punishment of the people of Nuh?

A) drowning

B) an earthquake

C) a volcano

167- What was the punishment of the people of Hud?

A) an electrocution

B) a devastating wind

C) a deluge of stones

168- Which sign God sent to Thamud?

A) a camel

B) a snake

C) a cow

169- Which people was Shouayb sent to?

A) 'Ad

B) Thamūd

C) Madyan

170- Which prophet could interpret dreams?

A) Zakaria (Zechariah)

B) Yusef (Joseph)

C) Hud (Eber)

171- Which prophet was afflicted in his goods, health and children?

A) Yussef (Joseph)

B) Yaa'qub (Jacob)

C) Ayub (Job)

172- Where did Musa (Moses) receive the revelation of his prophecy?

A) Mount Sinai

B) Mount Al-Nour

C) Mount Arafa

173- Which prophet was swallowed by a whale?

A) Yunes (Jonah)

B) Zakaria (Zechariah)

C) Saleh

174- Who did God assign beside Musa (Moses) to strengthen him throughout his mission?

A) His mother

B) His brother Harun (Aaron)

C) His sister

175- Who is the last messenger of all messengers?

A) Muhammad

B) Musa (Moses)

C) Isa (Jesus)

176- Where was the prophet Yunus (Jonah) confined during three days?

A) in prison

B) at the bottom of a well

C) in the belly of a whale

177- Which two miracles Musa (Moses) carried with him when he went to Pharaoh?

A) The stick and the hand

B) The camel and the cow

C) The wind and the birds

178- Who was the mother of the prophet Is-haq (Isaac)?

A) Hind

B) Sarah

C) Hajer

179- Who were the two sons of Adam?

A) Ismail et Is-haq

B) Habil (Abel) et Kabil (Caïn)

C) Quassim et Abdullah

180- Which prophet whose wife and son died by drowning?

A) Yunes (Jonah)

B) Musa (Moses)

C) Nuh (Noah)

181- Where was the prophet Yusuf thrown when he was a child and who did it?

A) in a well by his brothers

B) in a cave by brigands

C) in a river by his father

182- What happened to the prophet Ibrahim (Abraham) when his enemies threw him into fire?

A) The fire goes out by itself

B) The fire didn't burn Ibrahim

C) He died

183- Who was the mother of the prophet Ismail?

A) Hajer

B) Sarah

C) Zoulaikha

184- Which prophet had djinns in his service?

A) Sulayman (Solomon)

B) Ibrahim (Abraham)

C) Yusuf (Joseph)

185- Which people did the prophet Musa save?

A) The Thamūd

B) The Israelites

C) The Sodomites

186- Which prophet spoke directly to Allah?

A) Isa (Jesus)

B) Musa (Moses)

C) Muhammad

187- Which queen met the prophet Suleyman (Solomon)?

A) The queen of Egypt

B) The queen of Saba

C) The queen Victoria

188- Which prophet had a high ranked position in the king of Egypt's court?

A) Lut (Lot)

B) Musa (Moses)

C) Yusef (Joseph)

189- Who is the person that Musa has accompanied for some time?

A) Nuh (Noah)

B) Zakaria (Zechariah)

C) Al-Khadir

190- Which prophet was the nephew of the prophet Ibrahim?

A) Lut (Lot)

B) Dawud (David)

C) Suleyman (Solomon)

191- Which prophet was saved by a caravan and taken to Egypt?

A) Ismail

B) Yusuf (Joseph)

C) Yunes (Jonah)

192- Which prophet did Allah reveal the authentic Torah?

A) Musa (Moses)

B) Ayub (Job)

C) Isa (Jesus)

193- Which prophet did Allah grant the miracle of splitting the moon into two?

A) Yunes (Jonah)

B) Ilyes

C) Muhammad

194- How many prophets are mentioned in the Koran?

A) 20

B) 25

C) 30

195- Which prophet is living in the 2nd heaven now?

A) Isa (Jesus)

B) Musa (Moses)

C) Muhammad

196- For how long did the prophet Nuh (Noah) call his people to believe in God?

A) 500 years

B) 700 years

C) 950 years

197- Who was the oldest among the sons of Nuh?

A) Canaan

B) Sem

C) Japhet

198- Which prophet crossed the sea which was open to him and his people?

A) Saleh

B) Hud (Eber)

C) Musa (Moses)

199- Which prophet Allah revealed the Koran to?

A) Muhammad

B) Ilyes

C) Yunes (Jonah)

200- Who was the orator of the prophets?

A) Shou'ayb

B) Is-haq (Isaac)

C) Yaa'qub (Jacob)

THEME 4: General Knowledge in Islam

201- What does the word « Islam » mean?

A) Adoration

B) Submission to Allah

C) Invocation and prayer

202- Which country Mecca is situated in?

A) Saudi Arabia

B) France

C) Iraq

203- What building do the Muslims pray in?

A) A church

B) A mosque

C) A synagogue

204- The Muslims have a special day. Which one?

A) Monday

B) Friday

C) Sunday

205- Which town in Saudi Arabia is nicknamed « The town of the prophet» ?

A) Jeddah

B) Ryadh

C) Medina

206- Which country belonged to the Arab-Muslim world of Al-Andalus?

A) France

B) Egypt

C) Spain

207- A minaret is ...

A) a beverage

B) a food reserve

C) the tour in which « al Muadhin » calls for prayer

208- The children go to « madrasa » which is ...

A) religious school

B) room for prayers

C) church

209- During the prayer, after Al-Fatiha, we recite ...

A) Surah Al-Kahf (The cavern)

B) Surah Al-Falaq (The Rising Dawn)

C) any surah or few verses

210- To convert to Islam, it is compulsory to testify « La Ilaha
illa Allah » What does this expression mean?

A) We have to invoke the prophets to adore Allah

B) There is no God worthy of worship except Allah

211- Which building do the Muslims turn around in Mecca?

A) The Kaaba

B) The Souk

C) The Clock

212- Which place in the Arab-Muslim towns allows the sale of
products?

A) The minbar

B) The minaret

C) The souk

213- During which month Muslims fast?

A) Rajab

B) Ramadan

C) Dhu al Hajja

214- It is a sunnah to... ?

A) talk

B) smile

C) listen

215- It is not allowed for a Muslim to get angry at one's brother more than...

A) 5 days

B) 3 days

C) 2 days

216- One of the preoccupations of the caliph Abu Bakr is...

A) fight those who refused to acquit Zakat (alms)

B) fight the Romans

C) fight the Persians

217- Which companion was nicknamed Al-Faruk (Who discerns the truth from falsehood)

A) Abou Taleb

B) Abou Bakr

C) Omar

218- The 4 sacred months are

A) Sha'aban, Ramadan, Shawal et Dhul-Qa'ada

B) Ramadan, Dhul-Qa'ada, Dhul-Hijja et Muharram

C) Dhul-Qa'ada, Dhul-Hijja, Muharram et Rajab

219- Sunna designates ...

A) The sayings and deeds of the prophet Muhammad (pbuh)

B) The sayings and deeds of the first caliphs in Islam

C) The sayings and deeds of the companions of the prophet Muhammad (pbuh)

220- The wife of the prophet Muhammad and the sister of the caliph Muawia Ibn Abi Sufyane?

A) Ramla (Um Habiba)

B) Aisha

C) Zaynab

221- Ali Ibn Abi Taleb was appointed a caliph after:

A) The assassination of the caliph Othman

B) The normal death of the caliph Othman

C) The resignation of the caliph Othman

222- Who do we have the right to swear on?

A) Allah

B) The messenger of Allah (pbuh)

C) The Kaaba

223- How many pillars is Islam based on?

A) 3

B) 4

C) 5

224- How many centuries are there between Adam and Nuh (Noah)?

A) 2

B) 5

C) 10

225- Who are the first ones that converted to Islam?

A) Kadija, Ali, Abu Bakr

B) Omar, Othmane, Khaled

C) Abou Taleb, Talha, Zubeir

226- How many days is it recommended to fast per week and what are they?

A) 4 : Monday, Tuesday, Saturday and Sunday

B) 3 : Tuesday, Friday and Saturday

C) 2 : Monday and Thursday

227- What shall we do in the three white days?

A) make prayers and invocations

B) fast

C) give the Zakat (alms)

228- Who are Yajouj et Majouj (Gog and Magog)?

A) They are humans who were buried in the earth

B) They are animals which will come to attack humans

C) They are peoples that the prophet banished from Mecca

229- What shall we say at the end of each prayer?

A) Nothing

B) Assalamu Alaykom

C) Astaghfirou Allah (33 times) Alhamdou lillah

(33 times) Allahou akbar (33 times)

230- Which Surah is recommended to be read on Friday?

A) Al-Nahl (The Bee)

B) Al-Kahf (The Cave)

C) Al-Bourouj (The Constellations)

231- Who are the 2 most well-known people in compiling hadith In Islam?

A) Muslim and Al-Albani

B) Al-Bukhari and Al-Bayhaqi

C) Al-Bukhari et Muslim

232- Muslims say « Assalamu Alaykom » to greet each other. What does it mean?

A) Hello

B) May peace be with you

C) I greet you with dignity my friend

233- Which country has the largest number of Muslims?

A) Iran

B) Turkey

C) Indonesia

234- Which of these Muslim majority countries is not part of the Arab world?

A) Iran

B) Algeria

C) Yemen

235- Which year of Hijra did the fast of Ramadan become compulsory?

A) First year of Hijra

B) Second year of Hijra

C) Third year of Hijra

236- The verses related to fasting in Ramadan are found in surah:

A) Al-Baqara (The Cow)

B) Al-Imran (The Family of Imran)

C) Al-Nisaa (The Women)

237- The month of Ramadan is the month of :

A) prayer

B) holy war

C) patience

238- What is the main virtue of fasting?

A) It allows the loss of weight

B) It allows to feel the hunger of the poor

C) it reinforces hope and peace

239- Ramadan is one of the most sacred months in Islam

A) True

B) False

240- It is advised to follow Ramadan with

A) 3 more days

B) 6 more days

C) 10 more days

241- The angel Malik is :

A) Guardian of lake Kawther

B) Guardian of hell

C) Guardian of the bridge Sirat

242- How many angels fought in the battle of Badr?

A) 100

B) 500

C) 3000

243- Who said: « Evil has touched me but you are the most Merciful of the merciful »

A) John the Baptist

B) Job

C) Jesus

244- What is the name of the people who welcomed the prophet in Medina after his departure from Mecca?

A) Ansars

B) Quraych

C) Banu Khuza'a

245- The two angels which do the interrogation in the tomb are

A) Munkir and Nakir

B) Qabil and Habil

C) Israfil and A'zrail

246- Who said: « O my dear father, do as you are commanded, you will find me, if God wills among those who endure »

A) Isaac

B) Ismail

C) Abraham

247- On the prophet's night journey to heaven, how many prayers were originally prescribed for Muslims?

A) 15

B) 25

C) 50

248- The angels :

A) are infallible in the execution of orders

B) are immortal

C) can transform into objects

249- Who said: « Don't leave me alone, Lord, while You are The best of heirs »

A) Adam

B) Zechariah

C) Muhammad

250- Which of these animals don't have a surah in their names?

A) the ants

B) the birds

C) the bees

251- Which of these Surahs doesn't begin with letters?

A) Maryam (Mary)

B) Quraysh

C) Al-Kahf (The Cave)

252- Who said: « O my people, this is the camel of Allah that He sent to you as a sign. Let her graze in the land of Allah »

A) Shou'yab

B) Harun (Aaron)

C) Saleh

253- Who is the only companion whose name is mentioned in the Koran?

A) Abu Hurayra

B) Zayd Ibn Al Hareth

C) Bilal Ibn Rabah

254- The angel Israfil is charged with :

A) chaining the demons during Ramadan

B) blowing in the trunk on the day of resurrection

255- Before being Muslims, the Arabs were...

A) Polytheists

B) Monotheists

256- What is the departure of Muhammad from Mecca to Medina called?

A) Hijra

B) Hadith

C) Sunnah

257- Is prayer compulsory in Islam?

A) no

B) maybe

C) yes

258- Who said : « We believe in the Lord of the universe, the Lord of Moses and Aaron »

A) The guardians

B) The soldiers

C) The magicians

259- Angels are created from

A) fire

B) light

C) clay

260- According to what the prophet said, a strong man is the one who

A) is not afraid

B) knows how to fight

C) controls himself in moments of anger

261- Which wife of the prophet is known for reporting Hadiths?

A) Aicha

B) Zayneb

C) Khadija

262- Which is the 5th pillar in Islam?

A) prayer

B) Zakat (alms)

C) Hajj (pilgrimage)

263- How many pillars are there in faith?

A) 3

B) 5

C) 6

264- How many angels will carry the Throne of Allah on the Day of Judgment?

A) 50

B) 20

C) 8

265- Who said: « if you stretch out your hand to kill me, I Wouldn't stretch out my hand to kill you, because I fear Allah the Lord of the universe »

A) Ismail

B) Israil

C) Abel

266- The mission of the prophet Muhammad (pbuh) lasted...

A) 20 years

B) 23 years

C) 25 years

267- Who is known for his compilation of Hadiths (sayings of the prophet)?

A) Omar

B) Abdurrahmen

C) Al-Bukhari

268- On what basis is the practice of lending at interest (riba) condemned in Islam?

A) on two verses of the Koran

B) on two fatwas

C) on two hadiths

269- Why is the battle of Badr important?

A) It is the first victory won by Muslims against the Persians

B) It is the first victory won by Muslims against the Meccans

C) It is the first victory won by Muslims against the Byzantines

270- In which battle Aicha was defeated by Ali Ibn Abi Taleb?

A) The battle of Nahrawan

B) The battle of the Camel

C) The battle of Uhud

271- What year was the Hijra in?

A) 632 A.D

B) 622 A.D

C) 612 A.D

272- How do we call the religious, political and military leaders who followed Muhammad?

A) Emirs

B) Governors

C) Caliphs

273- Who said : « O my father, I saw eleven stars and also the sun and the moon, I saw them prostrate before me» ?

A) Joseph

B) Solomon

C) Abraham

274- What is the name of the dynasty of caliphs in place between 661 and 750?

A) The Abbassids

B) The Fatimids

C) The Umayyads

275- On what night was the Koran revealed?

A) The night of the nocturnal journey and the ascent

B) The night of destiny during the month of Ramadan

C) The night of the new year

276- How many sacred places are there in Islam?

A) 7

B) 1

C) 3

277- Where is the spiritual retreat done (ii'tikaf)?

A) on the Mont Blanc

B) in Medina

C) in the mosque

278- Who said: « O my Lord, show Yourself to me so that I may see You?

A) Adam

B) Moses

C) Jesus

279- How many times do we prostrate during the prayer of funeral?

A) Not once

B) Once

C) Twice

280- At which time of the day during the month of Ramadan do we stop the fast?

A) at midday

B) at midnight

C) just after the sunset

281- How do we call the art of writing beautiful letters?

A) literature

B) calligraphy

C) lexicography

282- How many wives did the prophet have?

A) 11

B) 7

C) 4

283- How many prophets are mentioned in the Koran?

A) 20

B) 25

C) 55

284- According to Allah, is there a difference between an Arab and a non-Arab?

A) Yes, depending on the breed

B) Yes, depending on the social class

C) No, just by piety

285- Who said : «O Adam, shall I point to you the tree of eternity and an imperishable kingdom »

A) Eve

B) Ibliss

C) Gabriel

286- How many verses does the longest surah in the Koran have?

A) 211

B) 286

C) 290

287- Have angels ever disobeyed the orders of Allah?

A) Yes, rarely

B) No, never

C) it depends on the mission

288- What words should a Muslim say when he is dying?

A) Astaghfirullah

B) Alhamdulillah

C) La ilaha ila Allah

289- Indicate 3 Holy cities in Islam

A) Mecca, Medina, Dubaï

B) Mecca, Medina, Jerusalem

C) Mecca, Medina, Manama

290- Who said: « Lord, show me how You resuscitate the dead »

A) Muhammad

B) Jesus

C) Abraham

291- On which day will the end of times occur?

A) Friday

B) Monday

C) Thursday

292- What is the most serious of sins?

A) neglect the prayer

B) association with Allah

C) the murder

293- How many wings does the angel Gabriel have?

A) 100

B) 200

C) 600

294- In the Muslim calendar (the lunar calendar), how many days are there in a month?

A) 29 to 30 days

B) 30 to 31 days

C) 28 to 29 days

295- Who said: « Didn't I say that you wouldn't keep patience with me »

A) Khidhr

B) Luqman

C) Imran

296- How many days does a Hegirian year count?

A) from 354 to 355 days

B) from 300 to 301 days

C) from 365 to 366 days

297- Which woman is considered the most knowledgeable in terms of religion?

A) Aicha Bint Abi Bakr

B) Khadija Bint Khuwayled

C) Asma Bint Abi Bakr

298- To which city was the emigration of Meccan Muslims?

A) Damascus

B) Casablanca

C) Abyssinia

299- Before establishing the Kaaba as a direction of prayer, what was the prayer direction of Muslims?

A) The mosque Quba

B) The mosque Al-Aqsa

C) The mosque of the prophet

300- What is the name of the Christian king who led an army to destroy the Kaaba?

A) Abraha

B) Behanzin

C) Caesar

Solutions

THEME 1: The Holy Koran

1- The first word revealed in the Koran " Iqraa" means:

A) pray

B) read

C) obey me

2- The word Koran means

A) Wisdom

B) Reading

C) Submission

3- What was the first language of the original version of the Holy Koran?

A) French

B) English

C) Arabic

4- A surah of the Koran is a set of :

A) letters

B) verses

C) Islamic teachings

5- The Holy Koran contains

A) 99 suras

B) 111 suras

C) 114 suras

6- How many Hizbs are there in the Koran?

A) 100

B) 60

C) 50

7- The revelation of the Koran was spread over :

A) 10 years

B) 15 years

C) 23 years

8- The revelation of the Koran took place in :

A) Mecca

B) Mecca and Medina

C) Mecca and in Mesopotamia

9- The revelations were done :

A) by surah

B) by 2 verses

C) in a variable way

10- The Holy Koran contains several parts (juz'). How many?

A) 30

B) 50

C) 70

11- Reading a surah is equivalent to reading one third of the Holy Koran. Which one?

A) Al-Ikhlaas

B) Al-Fatiha

C) Al-Baqarah

12- Which sura includes The Verse of Throne (Ayat al Kursi), known for its power of protection and healing?

A) Al-Baqarah

B) Al-Isra'a

13- The first sura of the Holy Koran is

A) Al-Fatiha

B) Al Baqarah

C) Al Hajj

14- The Holy Koran was revealed to the prophet (pbuh) during the month of :

A) Ramadan

B) Safar

C) Muharram

15- The Koran is the word of :

A) Gabriel

B) Allah

C) Muhammad

16- The Koran was descended to Muhammad (pbuh) by the angel ...

A) Israfil

B) Mikhail

C) Jibril (Gabriel)

17- How many verses are there in the Koran?

A) 4444

B) 6346

C) 5555

18- In the Koran, it was written that Allah pardons everyone except

A) Hypocrites

B) Polytheists

19- Which sura is the shortest one in the Koran?

A) Al-Baqarah

B) Al-Insan

C) Al-Kawthar

20- The longest sura in the Koran is ...

A) Al-Maida'a

B) Al-Baqarah

C) Al-Nissa

21- Which one is the only sura that does not contain "bismillah al Rahman al Rahim" at the beginning?

A) At-Tawbah

B) Maryam

22- The prophet who was mentioned 139 times in the Koran is ...

A) Ibrahim (Abraham)

B) Musa (Moses)

C) Issa (Jesus)

23- Which suras are full of light (Azzahrawen)?

   A) Al-Baqarah & Aal-Imran

   B) Al-Baqarah & At-Tawba

   C) Al-Nisa'a & Aal-Imran

24- Does The Koran only address Arabs?

   A) Yes

   B) No, the whole mankind

   C) Only the men

25- How many Meccan suras and Medina suras is the Koran composed of?

   A) 100 Meccan suras et 14 Medina suras

   B) 86 Meccan suras et 28 Medina suras

26- How many words does the Holy Koran consist of?

   A) 88439

   B) 77439

   C) 99439

27- How many letters are there in the Koran?

   A) 323670

   B) 556892

   C) 725874

28- How many "Sajda" does the Koran consist of?

   A) 10

   B) 12

   C) 14

29- A sura bears the name of one of the pillars of Islam. Which one?

   A) At-Tawba

B) Al-Hajj

C) Aal Imran

30- Which sura was named after one of the names of the Koran?

A) Al-Forqan

B) Al-Tawba

C) Al-Nour

31- A sura bears the name of a woman. Which one?

A) Mariem (Mary)

B) Rouquaya

C) Fatima

32- A sura contains bismillah twice. Which one?

A) Al-Nour

B) Al-Namel

C) At-Tawba

33- Which sura is named after one of the days of the week?

A) Al Baquarah

B) Al A'araf

C) Al Joumou'a (Friday)

34- Two surahs indicate two prayer times. Which ones?

A) Al-Sobeh et Al-Dhur

B) Al-Maghreb et Al-I'cha

C) Al-Fajr et Al-A'ser

35- A surah bears the name of a fruit. Which one?

A) Al-Tin (fig)

B) Al-Kawthar

C) Al-Ikhlas

36- A surah bears the name of a river. Which one?

A) Al-Kawther

B) Al-Ma'oun

C) Al-Falaq

37- Which surah bears the name of a planet?

A) Al-Kamar (Moon)

B) Al-Shams (Sun)

C) Al-Najm (Star)

38- How many words does "Ayat al Kursi" contain?

A) 30

B) 40

C) 50

39- Where were revealed the first verses of the Koran?

A) in the cave of Hira in Mecca

B) in Jerusalem

C) in Medina

40- Which sura equals to one fourth of the Koran?

A) Al-Kafiroun

B) Al-Ma'oun

41- A surah that initiates the Holy Koran is...

A) Al-Fatiha (The Opening)

B) Al-Nisaa (The Women)

C) Al-Baquara (The Cow)

42- When was the Koran revealed to the prophet Muhammad (pbuh)?

A) at the night of Destiny

B) at Aid-Al-Adhha (the festival of Sacrifice)

C) on the 10th day of Muharram

43- Which surah is called "the half of the Koran"?

A) Al-Zalzala (The Earthquake)

B) Al-Moutafifin (The dealers in Fraud)

C) Al-Houmaza (The Scandalmongers)

44- Which surah finished with two names of prophets?

    A.   Al-Nassr (The Victory)

B) Al-Massad (The Palm Fiber)

C) Al-A'ala (The All-Highest)

45- Which surah did not begin with bismillah?

A) At-Tawba (The Repentance)

B) A-Ikhlas (The Purity of Faith)

C) Al-Anbia'a (The prophets)

46- Which surah was revealed complete?

A) Al-Mudather (The Cloaked One)

B) Al-Ma'idah (The Table)

C) Al-Anbia'a (The prophets)

47- A Surah is named after one of the prophet's battles. Which one?

A) Al-Ahzeb (The Clans)

B) Al-Israa (The Night Journey)

48- Which surah was revealed to the prophet after his migration to Medina?

A) Al-Anfal (The Spoils of War)

B) Taha

C) Al-Baqarah (The Cow)

49- Which numbers are the most repeated in the Holy Koran?

A) 1 - 7

B) 5 - 11

C) 100 - 300

50- Which surah finished with the same word as its name?

A) Al-Kafiroun (The Disbelievers)

B) Al-Nas (The Mankind)

C) Al-Sharh (The Solace)

THEME 2 : The Prophet Muhammad

51- Where was Muhammad born?

A) in Medina

B) in Mecca

C) in Jerusalem

52- When did Muhammad live?

A) IV-V century

B) VI-VII century

C) VIII-IX century

53- What was the job of Muhammad?

A) Doctor

B) Shepherd

C) Lawyer

54- Who was his first wife?

A) Khadija

B) Fatima

C) Sarah

55- Where did Muhammad take refuge after his escape from Mecca?

A) Medina

B) Jerusalem

C) Damascus

56- Which people does Mouhammad take part of?

A) The Byzantines

B) The Francs

C) The Arabs

57- Where did Muhammad receive the word of God for the first time?

A) The Heet Cave

B) The Hira Cave

C) The Thor Cave

58- How do we call the successors of Muhammad?

A) Caliphs

B) Emirs

C) Sultans

59-   He heard ...

A) The words of Jesus

B) The words of his father

C) The words of Allah

60-   Did Muhammad know his parents?

A) Yes

B) No, he was an orphan

C) Maybe

61-   The prophet Muhammad (pbuh) was born in

A) 600 A.D

B) 570 A.D

62-   What is the name of Muhammad's father?

A) Abde Allah

B) Abou Bakr

63-   Which one is the name of Muhammad's mother?

A) Amina

B) Khadija

C) Fatima

64-   Did Muhammad's father die before or after the birth of the prophet Muhammad (pbuh)?

A) before his birth

B) after his birth

65-   The mother of the prophet Muhammad (pbuh) passed away when Muhammad was six years old?

A) True

B) False

66- The prophet Muhammad (pbuh) was eight years old when his grandfather died?

A) True

B) False

67- Which one is the name of the prophet's wet nurse?

A) Aïcha

B) Halima

68- Muhammad travelled to Cham (= Now Syria and parts of the neighboring countries) for the first time with his uncle at the age of ten?

A) True

B) False

69- After the death of his mother, he was adopted by his grandfather and then by his uncle.

A) True

B) False

70- The prophet started working as a shepherd

A) True

B) False

71- How old was he when Angel Jibril (Gabriel) first visited him?

A) 30

B) 35

C) 40

72- Which one of these three people is the cousin of the prophet?

A) Abou Baker Sedik

B) Ali Ibn Abi Talib

C) Othmane Ibn Affene

73- The name of Muhammad's father is ...

A) Abdel Muttalib

B) Abdellah

C) Ibrahim

74- Who is not the uncle of the prophet?

A) Hamza

B) Abbes

C) Abou Oubayda

75- The prophet had...

A) 4 daughters et 3 sons (Fatima, Zeyneb, Roukaya, Oum Kalthoum, Quassim, Ibrahim, Abdellah)

B) 7 daughters et 2 sons

C) 10 daughters et 4 sons

76- Who fostered the prophet successively after the death of his parents?

A) Abdul Muttalib then Abou Talib

B) Abbes then Abou Talib

C) Hamza then Abou Talib

77- Which children did the prophet bring up?

A) Talha and Zoubayr

B) Al-Mughira and Muawiya

C) Ali and Zayd Ibn Haritha

78- Who is not one of the prophet's daughters?

A) Zeyneb

B) Roukaya

C) Maymouna

79- The prophet was buried next to ...

A) Abu Bakr and Omar

B) Othmane and Ali

C) Zeyneb and Fatima

80- What are the names of the prophet's parents?

A) Jaafer and Hafsa

B) Omar and Halima

C) Abdullah and Amina

81- At what age did he marry Khadija?

A) 30

B) 25

C) 40

82- How much time did he stay in Mecca before his migration?

A) 7

B) 9

C) 13

83- What was his first battle?

A) Badr

B) Uhud

84- Shall we love the prophet more than our own family?

A) Yes

B) No

85- How old was the prophet when the first signs of prophecy were discovered?

A) Since his birth

B) 6 years old by his uncle Abu Talib

C) 12 years old by a monk named Bahira

86- During how much time the call to Islam was done secretly?

A) 5 years

B) 3 years

C) 1 year

87- Which miracle did he bring to mankind?

A) The Koran

B) The Gospel

C) The Torah

88- Which house was the prophet buried in?

A) Fatima

B) Aicha

C) Khadija

89- Which tribe does the prophet belong to?

A) Kouraych

B) Badr

C) Uhud

90- What was the name of the last battle where the prophet attended?

A) Badr

B) Tabuk

C) Hunayn

91- What is the name of the mountain where the Hira Cave is situated?

A) Uhud

B) Al-Nur

C) Arafa

92- Who was the last wife of the prophet Muhammad?

A) Hafsa

B) Zeyneb

C) Maymouna

93- How many battles did the prophet attend?

A) 18

B) 27

C) 35

94- Which food is the most eaten by the prophet?

A) dates and water

B) bread

C) meat

95- How many times did the prophet go on a pilgrimage during his entire life?

A) 1

B) 3

C) 5

96- After ten years of his mission, the prophet lost two important people. Who are they?

A) his sons Qassim et Abdullah

B) his uncle Abu Talib and his wife Khadija

C) his grandfather Abdul Muttalib and his uncle Abu Talib

97- Who is the most harmful person to the prophet?

A) Abu Lahab

B) Abu Sofien

C) Muawiya

98- What were the prophet's companions doing after 5 years of his mission?

A) They built a mosque in Medina

B) They said goodbye to their families

C) They migrated to Al Habacha (Abyssinia)

99- The prophet went on two great trips. Which ones?

A) Mecca and Medina

B) Israa et Miraj

C) Cham et Egypt

100- The prophet passed away at

A) 50

B) 63

C) 70

THEME 3: The prophets

101- Which prophet had the most detailed and beautiful story in the Koran?

A) Ismail

B) Yussef (Joseph)

C) Ibrahim (Abraham)

102- Which people was the prophet Saleh (Methuselah) sent to?

A) Thamūd

B) 'Ad

C) Madyan

103- Which prophet was nicknamed the father of hosts (Abu Ad Dayfan)?

A) Nuh (Noah)

B) Ibrahim (Abraham)

C) Suleyman (Solomon)

104- Which birds did God send to Kabil (Cain) after he had killed his brother Habil (Abel)?

A) eagles

B) crows

C) swans

105- God said: « And we raised him to a high rank ». Which prophet is this?

A) Ismail (Ishmael)

B) Isa (Jesus)

C) Idris (Enoch)

106- How many stars did the prophet Yusuf see in his dream?

A) 9

B) 10

C) 11

107- Which prophet was the first one to make chainmail?

A) Dawud (David)

B) Zakariya (Zechariah)

C) Nuh (Noah)

108-　Which prophet spoke to people in his cradle?

A) Ilyas (Elijah)

B) Musa (Moses)

C) Isa (Jesus)

109-　Who was the Torah revealed to?

A) Isa (Jesus)

B) Musa (Moses)

C) Dawud (David)

110-　How many nights since the beginning of Ramadan have the psalms been revealed to David?

A) 6

B) 12

C) 21

111-　Who is the prophet with whom King Nemrod was having a discussion?

A) Suleyman (Solomon)

B) Musa (Moses)

C) Ibrahim (Abraham)

112-　The richest and the most powerful prophet is..

A) Suleyman (Solomon)

B) Musa (Moses)

C) Ibrahim (Abraham)

113-　The poorest prophet is ...

A) Musa (Moses)

B) Ibrahim (Abraham)

C) Isa (Jesus)

114-　The prophet whose name was drawn from God Himself is ...

A) Ibrahim (Abraham)

B) Musa (Moses)

C) Muhammad

115-   The prophet whose name means vitality (His parents were aged)

A) Yahya (John the Baptist)

B) Ibrahim (Abraham)

C) Isa (Jesus)

116-   The most mentioned prophet in the Koran is:

A) Ibrahim (Abraham)

B) Musa (Moses)

C) Isa (Jesus)

117-   The prophet who was abandoned by his ten brothers was...

A) Ibrahim (Abraham)

B) Isa (Jesus)

C) Yusuf (Joseph)

118-   The prophet who was about to be sacrificed and helped to build the Kaaba is ...

A) Ismail (Ishmael)

B) Ibrahim (Abraham)

C) Yusuf (Joseph)

119-   God has blessed him on the day of his birth, his death and when he will resuscitate

A) Yahya (John the Baptist)

B) Isa (Jesus)

C) Ibrahim (Abraham)

120-   The prophet whose people were destroyed after a deluge of stones is ...

A) Musa (Moses)

B) Ibrahim (Abraham)

C) Lut (Lot)

121-   The prophet whose people were destroyed by a deluge

A) Dawud (David)

B) Musa (Moses)

C) Nuh (Noah)

122-   The prophet whose people threw him into fire

A) Ibrahim (Abraham)

B) Nuh (Noah)

C) Ismail (Ishmael)

123-   Who was the first messenger on earth?

A) Nuh (Noah)

B) Adam

C) Ibrahim (Abraham)

124-   Musa (Moses), Harun (Aaron), Mariam (Mary) are the children of...

A) Yaa'qub (Jacob)

B) Imran

C) Ilyas

125-   Which prophet was sent to the people of 'Ad?

A) Idris (Enoch)

B) Isa (Jesus)

C) Hud (Eber)

126-   Which prophet who had food coming out of his finger, when being a child?

A) Musa (Moses)

B) Shu'ayb

C) Ibrahim (Abraham)

127-   Which animal was supposed to eat Yusuf (Joseph)?

A) a camel

B) a wolf

C) a cow

128- Which prophet spoke directly to Allah?

A) Ibrahim (Abraham)

B) Musa (Moses)

C) Isa (Jesus)

129- Which prophet underwent most ordeals?

A) Dawud (David)

B) Suleyman (Solomon)

C) Ayub (Job)

130- Which prophet whose the beauty equals to half of the mankind?

A) Yusef (Joseph)

B) Lut (Lot)

C) Nuh (Noah)

131- Which prophet was the friend of Allah?

A) Idris (Enoch)

B) Ibrahim (Abraham)

C) Musa (Moses)

132- Which prophet had a night journey, visited the 7 heavens and saw the prophets?

A) Ibrahim (Abraham)

B) Muhammad (pbuh)

C) Isa (Jesus)

133- Which prophet died in the 4th sky?

A) Hud

B) Imran

C) Idris (Enoch)

134- How many times did Muhammad (pbuh) see Jibril (Gabriel) in his angelic figure?

A) 7

B) 2

C) 17

135-   How many prophets and messengers are there overall?

A) 100

B) 1000

C) 124000

136-   Which prophet did «Bani Israel» cut into two pieces?

A) Zakaria (Zechariah)

B) Yahya (John the Baptist)

C) Musa (Moses)

137-   Which prophet ate the leaves in fear of falling into the sin?

A) Musa (Moses)

B) Yahya (John the Baptist)

C) Isa (Jesus)

138-   How many sons does Ya'qub (Jacob) have?

A) 11

B) 12

C) 13

139-   Yaa'qub is the father of Jews

A) False

B) True

C) we don't know

140-   Who is the father of the prophets?

A) Adam

B) Ibrahim (Abraham)

C) Muhammad

141-   Who is our teacher on earth?

A) Adam

B) Muhammad

C) Isa (Jesus)

142- Today, we are the children of ...

A) Adam

B) Muhammad

C) Ibrahim (Abraham)

143- There is a rock in Palestine where were killed ...

A) 50 prophets

B) 70 prophets

C) 100 from Bani Israël

144- The prophets are all messengers

A) False

B) True

C) We don't know

145- Which prophet made the believers cross the Red Sea and saved them from Pharaoh?

A) Nuh (Noah)

B) Ibrahim (Abraham)

C) Musa (Moses)

146- Which prophet was evicted from his house by his 11 brothers by jealousy and was bought as a
slave in Egypt?

A) Yahya (John the Baptist)

B) Yusuf (Joseph)

C) Nuh (Noah)

147- Who is the prophet Isa?

A) Jesus, son of Mary

B) Musa (Moses)

C) Ibrahim (Abraham)

148- Which prophet built an ark in order to gather the believers In God?

A) Idriss (Enoch)

B) Ismaïl (Ishmael)

C) Nuh (Noah)

149-   Which prophets built "Al-Kaaba" in Mecca?

A) Ayub (Jacob) et Idris (Enoch)

B) Ibrahim (Abraham) et Ismail (Ishmael)

C) Nuh (Noah) et Saleh (Methuselah)

150-   Which prophet was the cousin of the prophet Yahya (John the Baptist)?

A) Yunes (Jonah)

B) Isa (Jesus)

C) Yaa'qub (Jacob)

151-   Ibrahim (Abraham) had two sons that were prophets, who are they?

A) Ismail et Is-haq (Isaac)

B) Adam et Eve

C) Yunus (Jonah) et Hud (Eber)

152-   Which prophet underwent the affliction of a long and painful illness?

A) Muhammad

B) Saleh

C) Ayub (Job)

153-   Which prophet was the son of the prophet Dawud (David)?

A) Musa (Moses)

B) Yussef (Joseph)

C) Suleyman (Solomon)

154-   The miracle of the camel was granted to

A) Adam

B) Idris (Enoch)

C) Saleh

155-   In Islam, who was the last prophet sent to the whole mankind?

A) Isa (Jesus)

B) Muhammad

C) Yunus (Jonah)

156-   The prophet who had leprosy was ...

A) Ayub (Job)

B) Saleh

C) Adam

157-   The most mentioned prophet in the Koran is

A) Muhammad

B) Musa (Moses)

C) Isa (Jesus)

158-   The prophet whose people were destroyed by deluge of stones is

A) Lut (Lot)

B) Hud (Eber)

C) Dawud (David)

159-   Which prophet has never lied except 3 times

A) Ibrahim (Abraham)

B) Ismail

C) Is-haq (Isaac)

160-   Which prophet knew how to speak to birds?

A) Lut (Lot)

B) Dawud (David)

C) Suleyman (Solomon)

161-   For how long did the prophet Ayub (Job) endure his affliction?

A) 12 years

B) 18 years

C) 21 years

162-   Which prophet was a carpenter?

A) Zakaria (Zachariah)

B) Yahya (John the Baptist)

C) Is-haq (Isaac)

163- Which prophet was sent to a people who were struck by an earthquake for calling him a liar?

A) Is-haq (Isaac)

B) Yaa'qub (Jacob)

C) Shou'ayb (Jethro)

164- Which prophet Ibliss refused to prostrate?

A) Adam

B) Nuh (Noah)

C) Musa (Moses)

165- Who was the first messenger?

A) Dawud (David)

B) Ibrahim (Abraham)

C) Nuh (Noah)

166- What was the punishment of the people of Nuh?

A) drowning

B) an earthquake

C) a volcano

167- What was the punishment of the people of Hud?

A) an electrocution

B) a devastating wind

C) a deluge of stones

168- Which sign God sent to Thamud?

A) a camel

B) a snake

C) a cow

169- Which people was Shouayb sent to?

A) 'Ad

B) Thamūd

C) Madyan

170- Which prophet could interpret dreams?

A) Zakaria (Zechariah)

B) Yusef (Joseph)

C) Hud (Eber)

171- Which prophet was afflicted in his goods, health and children?

A) Yussef (Joseph)

B) Yaa'qub (Jacob)

C) Ayub (Job)

172- Where did Musa (Moses) receive the revelation of his prophecy?

A) Mount Sinai

B) Mount Al-Nour

C) Mount Arafa

173- Which prophet was swallowed by a whale?

A) Yunes (Jonah)

B) Zakaria (Zechariah)

C) Saleh

174- Who did God assign beside Musa (Moses) to strengthen him throughout his mission?

A) His mother

B) His brother Harun (Aaron)

C) His sister

175- Who is the last messenger of all messengers?

A) Muhammad

B) Musa (Moses)

C) Isa (Jesus)

176- Where was the prophet Yunus (Jonah) confined during three days?

A) in prison

B) at the bottom of a well

C) in the belly of a whale

177- Which two miracles Musa (Moses) carried with him when he went to Pharaoh?

A) The stick and the hand

B) The camel and the cow

C) The wind and the birds

178- Who was the mother of the prophet Is-haq (Isaac)?

A) Hind

B) Sarah

C) Hajer

179- Who were the two sons of Adam?

A) Ismail et Is-haq

B) Habil (Abel) et Kabil (Caïn)

C) Quassim et Abdullah

180- Which prophet whose wife and son died by drowning?

A) Yunes (Jonah)

B) Musa (Moses)

C) Nuh (Noah)

181- Where was the prophet Yusuf thrown when he was a child and who did it?

A) in a well by his brothers

B) in a cave by brigands

C) in a river by his father

182- What happened to the prophet Ibrahim (Abraham) when his enemies threw him into fire?

A) The fire goes out by itself

B) The fire didn't burn Ibrahim

C) He died

183- Who was the mother of the prophet Ismail?

A) Hajer

B) Sarah

C) Zoulaikha

184- Which prophet had djinns in his service?

A) Sulayman (Solomon)

B) Ibrahim (Abraham)

C) Yusuf (Joseph)

185- Which people did the prophet Musa save?

A) The Thamūd

B) The Israelites

C) The Sodomites

186- Which prophet spoke directly to Allah?

A) Isa (Jesus)

B) Musa (Moses)

C) Muhammad

187- Which queen met the prophet Suleyman (Solomon)?

A) The queen of Egypt

B) The queen of Saba

C) The queen Victoria

188- Which prophet had a high ranked position in the king of Egypt's court?

A) Lut (Lot)

B) Musa (Moses)

C) Yusef (Joseph)

189- Who is the person that Musa has accompanied for some time?

A) Nuh (Noah)

B) Zakaria (Zechariah)

C) Al-Khadir

190- Which prophet was the nephew of the prophet Ibrahim?

A) Lut (Lot)

B) Dawud (David)

C) Suleyman (Solomon)

191- Which prophet was saved by a caravan and taken to Egypt?

A) Ismail

B) Yusuf (Joseph)

C) Yunes (Jonah)

192- Which prophet did Allah reveal the authentic Torah?

A) Musa (Moses)

B) Ayub (Job)

C) Isa (Jesus)

193- Which prophet did Allah grant the miracle of splitting the moon into two?

A) Yunes (Jonah)

B) Ilyes

C) Muhammad

194- How many prophets are mentioned in the Koran?

A) 20

B) 25

C) 30

195- Which prophet is living in the 2nd heaven now?

A) Isa (Jesus)

B) Musa (Moses)

C) Muhammad

196- For how long did the prophet Nuh (Noah) call his people to believe in God?

A) 500 years

B) 700 years

C) 950 years

197-   Who was the oldest among the sons of Nuh?

A) Canaan

B) Sem

C) Japhet

198-   Which prophet crossed the sea which was open to him and his people?

A) Saleh

B) Hud (Eber)

C) Musa (Moses)

199-   Which prophet Allah revealed the Koran to?

A) Muhammad

B) Ilyes

C) Yunes (Jonah)

200-   Who was the orator of the prophets?

A) Shou'ayb

B) Is-haq (Isaac)

C) Yaa'qub (Jacob)

THEME 4: General Knowledge in Islam

201- What does the word « Islam » mean?

A) Adoration

B) Submission to Allah

C) Invocation and prayer

202- Which country Mecca is situated in?

A) Saudi Arabia

B) France

C) Iraq

203- What building do the Muslims pray in?

A) A church

B) A mosque

C) A synagogue

204- The Muslims have a special day. Which one?

A) Monday

B) Friday

C) Sunday

205- Which town in Saudi Arabia is nicknamed « The town of the prophet» ?

A) Jeddah

B) Ryadh

C) Medina

206- Which country belonged to the Arab-Muslim world of Al-Andalus?

A) France

B) Egypt

C) Spain

207- A minaret is ...

A) a beverage

B) a food reserve

C) the tour in which « al Muadhin » calls for prayer

208- The children go to « madrasa » which is ...

A) religious school

B) room for prayers

C) church

209- During the prayer, after Al-Fatiha, we recite ...

A) Surah Al-Kahf (The cavern)

B) Surah Al-Falaq (The Rising Dawn)

C) any surah or few verses

210- To convert to Islam, it is compulsory to testify « La Ilaha illa Allah »
What does this expression
mean?

A) We have to invoke the prophets to adore Allah

B) There is no God worthy of worship except Allah

211- Which building do the Muslims turn around in Mecca?

A) The Kaaba

B) The Souk

C) The Clock

212- Which place in the Arab-Muslim towns allows the sale of products?

A) The minbar

B) The minaret

C) The souk

213- During which month Muslims fast?

A) Rajab

B) Ramadan

C) Dhu al Hajja

214- It is a sunnah to... ?

A) talk

B) smile

C) listen

215- It is not allowed for a Muslim to get angry at one's brother more than...

A) 5 days

B) 3 days

C) 2 days

216- One of the preoccupations of the caliph Abu Bakr is...

A) fight those who refused to acquit Zakat (alms)

B) fight the Romans

C) fight the Persians

217- Which companion was nicknamed Al-Faruk (Who discerns the truth from falsehood)

A) Abou Taleb

B) Abou Bakr

C) Omar

218- The 4 sacred months are

A) Sha'aban, Ramadan, Shawal et Dhul-Qa'ada

B) Ramadan, Dhul-Qa'ada, Dhul-Hijja et Muharram

C) Dhul-Qa'ada, Dhul-Hijja, Muharram et Rajab

219- Sunna designates ...

A) The sayings and deeds of the prophet Muhammad (pbuh)

B) The sayings and deeds of the first caliphs in Islam

C) The sayings and deeds of the companions of the prophet Muhammad (pbuh)

220- The wife of the prophet Muhammad and the sister of the caliph Muawia Ibn Abi Sufyane?

A) Ramla (Um Habiba)

B) Aisha

C) Zaynab

221-　Ali Ibn Abi Taleb was appointed a caliph after:

　　A) The assassination of the caliph Othman

　　B) The normal death of the caliph Othman

　　C) The resignation of the caliph Othman

222-　Who do we have the right to swear on?

　　A) Allah

　　B) The messenger of Allah (pbuh)

　　C) The Kaaba

223-　How many pillars is Islam based on?

　　A) 3

　　B) 4

　　C) 5

224-　How many centuries are there between Adam and Nuh (Noah)?

　　A) 2

　　B) 5

　　C) 10

225-　Who are the first ones that converted to Islam?

　　A) Kadija, Ali, Abu Bakr

　　B) Omar, Othmane, Khaled

　　C) Abou Taleb, Talha, Zubeir

226-　How many days is it recommended to fast per week and what are they?

　　A) 4 : Monday, Tuesday, Saturday and Sunday

　　B) 3 : Tuesday, Friday and Saturday

　　C) 2 : Monday and Thursday

227-　What shall we do in the three white days?

　　A) make prayers and invocations

　　B) fast

　　C) give the Zakat (alms)

228-　Who are Yajouj et Majouj (Gog and Magog)?

A) They are humans who were buried in the earth

B) They are animals which will come to attack humans

C) They are peoples that the prophet banished from Mecca

229- What shall we say at the end of each prayer?

A) Nothing

B) Assalamu Alaykom

C) Astaghfirou Allah (33 times) Alhamdou lillah (33 times) Allahou akbar (33 times)

230- Which Surah is recommended to be read on Friday?

A) Al-Nahl (The Bee)

B) Al-Kahf (The Cave)

C) Al-Bourouj (The Constellations)

231- Who are the 2 most well-known people in compiling hadith in Islam?

A) Muslim and Al-Albani

B) Al-Bukhari and Al-Bayhaqi

C) Al-Bukhari et Muslim

232- Muslims say « Assalamu Alaykom » to greet each other. What does it mean?

A) Hello

B) May peace be with you

C) I greet you with dignity my friend

233- Which country has the largest number of Muslims?

A) Iran

B) Turkey

C) Indonesia

234- Which of these Muslim majority countries is not part of the Arab world?

A) Iran

B) Algeria

C) Yemen

235- Which year of Hijra did the fast of Ramadan become compulsory?

A) First year of Hijra

B) Second year of Hijra

C) Third year of Hijra

236- The verses related to fasting in Ramadan are found in surah:

A) Al-Baqara (The Cow)

B) Al-Imran (The Family of Imran)

C) Al-Nisaa (The Women)

237- The month of Ramadan is the month of :

A) prayer

B) holy war

C) patience

238- What is the main virtue of fasting?

A) It allows the loss of weight

B) It allows to feel the hunger of the poor

C) it reinforces hope and peace

239- Ramadan is one of the most sacred months in Islam

A) True

B) False

240- It is advised to follow Ramadan with

A) 3 more days

B) 6 more days

C) 10 more days

241- The angel Malik is :

A) Guardian of lake Kawther

B) Guardian of hell

C) Guardian of the bridge Sirat

242- How many angels fought in the battle of Badr?

A) 100

B) 500

C) 3000

243- Who said: « Evil has touched me but you are the most Merciful of the merciful »

A) John the Baptist

B) Job

C) Jesus

244- What is the name of the people who welcomed the prophet in Medina after his departure from Mecca?

A) Ansars

B) Quraych

C) Banu Khuza'a

245- The two angels which do the interrogation in the tomb are

A) Munkir and Nakir

B) Qabil and Habil

C) Israfil and A'zrail

246- Who said : « O my dear father, do as you are commanded, you will find me, if God wills among those who endure »

A) Isaac

B) Ismail

C) Abraham

247- On the prophet's night journey to heaven, how many prayers were originally prescribed for Muslims?

A) 15

B) 25

C) 50

248- The angels :

A) are infallible in the execution of orders

B) are immortal

C) can transform into objects

249- Who said: « Don't leave me alone, Lord, while You are The best of heirs »

A) Adam

B) Zechariah

C) Muhammad

250- Which of these animals don't have a surah in their names?

A) the ants

B) the birds

C) the bees

251- Which of these Surahs doesn't begin with letters?

A) Maryam (Mary)

B) Quraysh

C) Al-Kahf (The Cave)

252- Who said: « O my people, this is the camel of Allah that He sent to you as a sign. Let her graze in the land of Allah »

A) Shou'yab

B) Harun (Aaron)

C) Saleh

253- Who is the only companion whose name is mentioned in the Koran?

A) Abu Hurayra

B) Zayd Ibn Al Hareth

C) Bilal Ibn Rabah

254- The angel Israfil is charged with :

A) chaining the demons during Ramadan

B) blowing in the trunk on the day of resurrection

255- Before being Muslims, the Arabs were...

A) Polytheists

B) Monotheists

256- What is the departure of Muhammad from Mecca to Medina called?

A) Hijra

B) Hadith

C) Sunnah

257- Is prayer compulsory in Islam?

A) no

B) maybe

C) yes

258- Who said : « We believe in the Lord of the universe, the Lord of Moses and Aaron »

A) The guardians

B) The soldiers

C) The magicians

259- Angels are created from

A) fire

B) light

C) clay

260- According to what the prophet said, a strong man is the one who

A) is not afraid

B) knows how to fight

C) controls himself in moments of anger

261- Which wife of the prophet is known for reporting Hadiths?

A) Aicha

B) Zayneb

C) Khadija

262- Which is the 5th pillar in Islam?

A) prayer

B) Zakat (alms)

C) Hajj (pilgrimage)

263- How many pillars are there in faith?

A) 3

B) 5

C) 6

264- How many angels will carry the Throne of Allah on the Day of Judgment?

A) 50

B) 20

C) 8

265- Who said: « if you stretch out your hand to kill me, I Wouldn't stretch out my hand to kill you,
because I fear Allah the Lord of the universe »

A) Ismail

B) Israil

C) Abel

266- The mission of the prophet Muhammad (pbuh) lasted...

A) 20 years

B) 23 years

C) 25 years

267- Who is known for his compilation of Hadiths (sayings of the prophet)?

A) Omar

B) Abdurrahmen

C) Al-Bukhari

268- On what basis is the practice of lending at interest (riba) condemned in Islam?

A) on two verses of the Koran

B) on two fatwas

C) on two hadiths

269- Why is the battle of Badr important?

A) It is the first victory won by Muslims against the Persians

B) It is the first victory won by Muslims against the Meccans

C) It is the first victory won by Muslims against the Byzantines

270- In which battle Aicha was defeated by Ali Ibn Abi Taleb?

A) The battle of Nahrawan

B) The battle of the Camel

C) The battle of Uhud

271- What year was the Hijra in?

A) 632 A.D

B) 622 A.D

C) 612 A.D

272- How do we call the religious, political and military leaders who followed Muhammad?

A) Emirs

B) Governors

C) Caliphs

273- Who said : « O my father, I saw eleven stars and also the sun and the moon, I saw them prostrate
before me »?

A) Joseph

B) Solomon

C) Abraham

274- What is the name of the dynasty of caliphs in place between 661 and 750?

A) The Abbassids

B) The Fatimids

C) The Umayyads

275- On what night was the Koran revealed?

A) The night of the nocturnal journey and the ascent

B) The night of destiny during the month of Ramadan

C) The night of the new year

276- How many sacred places are there in Islam?

A) 7

B) 1

C) 3

277- Where is the spiritual retreat done (ii'tikaf)?

A) on the Mont Blanc

B) in Medina

C) in the mosque

278- Who said: « O my Lord, show Yourself to me so that I may see You?

A) Adam

B) Moses

C) Jesus

279- How many times do we prostrate during the prayer of funeral?

A) Not once

B) Once

C) Twice

280- At which time of the day during the month of Ramadan do we stop the fast?

A) at midday

B) at midnight

C) just after the sunset

281- How do we call the art of writing beautiful letters?

A) literature

B) calligraphy

C) lexicography

282- How many wives did the prophet have?

A) 11

B) 7

C) 4

283- How many prophets are mentioned in the Koran?

A) 20

B) 25

C) 55

284- According to Allah, is there a difference between an Arab and a non-Arab?

A) Yes, depending on the breed

B) Yes, depending on the social class

C) No, just by piety

285- Who said : «O Adam, shall I point to you the tree of eternity and an imperishable kingdom »

A) Eve

B) Ibliss

C) Gabriel

286- How many verses does the longest surah in the Koran have?

A) 211

B) 286

C) 290

287- Have angels ever disobeyed the orders of Allah?

A) Yes, rarely

B) No, never

C) it depends on the mission

288- What words should a Muslim say when he is dying?

A) Astaghfirullah

B) Alhamdulillah

C) La ilaha ila Allah

289- Indicate 3 Holy cities in Islam

A) Mecca, Medina, Dubaï

B) Mecca, Medina, Jerusalem

C) Mecca, Medina, Manama

290- Who said: « Lord, show me how You resuscitate the dead »

A) Muhammad

B) Jesus

C) Abraham

291- On which day will the end of times occur?

A) Friday

B) Monday

C) Thursday

292- What is the most serious of sins?

A) neglect the prayer

B) association with Allah

C) the murder

293- How many wings does the angel Gabriel have?

A) 100

B) 200

C) 600

294- In the Muslim calendar (the lunar calendar), how many days are there in a month?

A) 29 to 30 days

B) 30 to 31 days

C) 28 to 29 days

295- Who said : « Didn't I say that you wouldn't keep patience with me »

A) Khidhr

B) Luqman

C) Imran

296- How many days does a Hegirian year count?

A) from 354 to 355 days

B) from 300 to 301 days

C) from 365 to 366 days

297- Which woman is considered the most knowledgeable in terms of religion?

A) Aicha Bint Abi Bakr

B) Khadija Bint Khuwayled

C) Asma Bint Abi Bakr

298- To which city was the emigration of Meccan Muslims?

A) Damascus

B) Casablanca

C) Abyssinia

299- Before establishing the Kaaba as a direction of prayer, what was the prayer direction of Muslims?

A) The mosque Quba

B) The mosque Al-Aqsa

C) The mosque of the prophet

300- What is the name of the Christian king who led an army to destroy the Kaaba?

A) Abraha

B) Behanzin

C) Caesar

Don't miss out!

Visit the website below and you can sign up to receive emails whenever WBwinner Publishing publishes a new book. There's no charge and no obligation.

https://books2read.com/r/B-A-ZSVDB-YKYWC

www.ingramcontent.com/pod-product-compliance
Lightning Source LLC
Chambersburg PA
CBHW052110150726
48002CB00006B/2297